The Elephant of Surprise

The Elephant of Surprise
prose poems

by Charles Harper Webb

MOON
TIDE PRESS

~ 2026 ~

The Elephant of Surprise
© Copyright 2026 Charles Harper Webb

Editor-in-chief
Eric Morago

Operations Associate
Shelly Holder

Associate Editors
Mackensi E. Green
Ellen Webre
Allysa Murray

Editor Emeritus
Michael Miller

Front cover art
Tyler Kinnaman

Author photo
Karen Schneider

Book design
Michael Wada

Moon Tide logo design
Abraham Gomez

The Elephant of Surprise
is published by Moon Tide Press

Moon Tide Press
6709 Washington Ave. #9297
Whittier, CA 90608
www.moontidepress.com

FIRST EDITION

Printed in the United States of America

ISBN #978-1-957799-47-6

CONTENTS

I

II

III

for Karen and Erik

The elephant of surprise is indispensable in a raid.

I

THE SECRET OF MY SUCCESS

I hate when poets say, "My poems write themselves."
— Overheard

After years of marching when I order, "March," and hurtling into hails of critics' lead when I yell, "Charge," my poems plop down by a brook in a mountain meadow, and won't budge.

"Change your titles," Epithalamion shouts. "They suck the mop."

"It's like you have a thousand kids named Enuresis," Poem brays.

"Worse than that!" pipes Meditation from the rear.

I work them over—sap and brass knucks—for a week, then hire an editor from the hardboiled avant-garde. "A Fleeting Thought" becomes "Galoshes For My Nose." "Composed After Long Grieving" becomes "Decomposed After Long Heaving."

"Let's go," I yell. "We've got landscapes to describe using scholarly allusions and words like *crinkum-crankum* with superb mouth-feel. We've got family contretemps and social inequities that, boxed in loose hexameter, will win us grants and get us in *Morton's Anthology*."

My poems double-time forward, but stop outside a store in which the sales staff—all Scottish terriers—sell nothing but popped Valentine balloons.

"We hate where you send us," the poems whine. "We want to go where *we* want to go."

I cyanide their rations and phosgene whole manuscripts, to no avail. My "Variations on a Coffee Stain in the *New Yorker*" turns into "Damp Jemima," a lament that home-made pancakes never taste as good as the restaurant kind. My saga "Wittgenstein" re-invents itself as a haiku on sumo wrestling, "The Great Fatsby."

"Armies have discipline," I rage. "You're a mob. A rout of savages. A murder of iambs!" Finally, though, like a parent whose kids, despite Bach in the bassinet, and ten years of charm school, become crack-whores, stoat-swallowers, and dog phrenologists, I tell my poems, "I quit. You're on your own."

ONLY SO MUCH PATIENCE

"A man has only so much patience," growls Beethoven.

"He must have more," the Universe replies.

"If he had more, he wouldn't have only so much," barks Beethoven.

"Then he must wait impatiently," the Universe declares.

"Why aren't his wishes granted?! Why must he wait at all?!" bellows Beethoven.

"He has no choice," the Universe explains.

"He has a choice," thunders Beethoven. "He just can't prove he does."

"Choose then, and leave me in peace," the Universe roars.

"Fine. I'll write tunes for a while, go deaf and die," Beethoven cries.

HALLOWEEN

"Don't tell me you're going out in *that*."

Harold drops the black cape draped around his shoulders. Plastic fangs fall to the floor as he protests, "Why not? I was a hit last year."

His wife, Denise, shapes a dab of sour cream on her forehead. "Old news. The thing to be this year is food."

"If you like being a Monterrey tostada, fine," Harold says. "I like being Dracula."

"It's so regressive," Denise says. "Helen's going as a ham-and-cheese on rye, Jack's going as a jello salad, Barbara's going as a knackwurst. Wei Ming's going as either Almond Chicken or Moo Shu Pork . . ."

"What ever happened to monsters and ballerinas?"

"It has to do with demolishing Eurocentric assumptions or post-colonialism or something. It's all over the news."

"I hate the news. It's depressing."

"See? Neglect your social responsibility, and the world leaves you behind."

She points to a huge hotdog bun stretched out on the couch. "Slip into this. You're Polish. Be a kielbasa."

"I'm only a fourth Polish. I hate kielbasa."

"Well, squeeze some lemon on your head, and go as a broiled trout."

"I'm allergic to fish."

"Okay—put these on and be a baked potato. You love those."

Grumbling, Harold steps between the giant potato skins Denise drags out of the closet. They close around him "like a damn Venus fly-trap. It'll take the Jaws of Life to extract me," he mutters, following Denise out under the silver-platter-moon, into the crisp-as-a-green-salad autumn air.

ESQUIRE

Charged with raising poultry without a permit, David Ashley appeared in court in Seneca Falls, NY, with a rooster. Asked to remove it, he said it was his attorney.
— News of the Weird

It was tough being the sole student glad to work for chicken feed.

"Millet's fine with me," he'd *bwock* as classmates scarfed his relatives, rolled in spice and citrus marinade.

How he loathed humans: the comb-less males, their feathers limp as rain-soaked worms; the cow-hipped, chattering hens, desperate to make every male mount only *one* of them; the lies that spewed out of all their fleshy beaks full of dull knives designed to torture as they chewed.

"People call cowards, *chicken;* bad hand-writing, *chicken-scratch;* bad behavior, *chicken shit.* Right in front of me!" he wrote in his diary. "Dr. Hawke told me, *Stop running around like your head's cut off, bird-brain.* You think the ACLU gives a cluck?!"

"I'll show them all," he squawked each morning, memorizing case law instead of greeting the day—writing briefs instead of cock-of-the-walking hen to hen, feathers flaming in the sun.

Only when, perched on the podium for his valedictory address, he saw the other students stuffed tight with dismay, did the glory of his victory, in shades of green and gold and purple, dawn. Then, precedent be damned, didn't he crow!

CONCEALED CARRY

In line at the Post Office, I'm swooping my tortoise like a fighter jet when a policeman grabs my arm. "You're busted for no turtle, Perp," he says.

Nationwide, turtles are under attack: waiting periods; restrictions on who can buy, and how many; one box of food-pellets per week, maximum. To counter that, our City Council made it illegal *not* to carry one.

I hold mine out so the officer can feel its shell and squeeze its armored feet.

"Don't raise your fist at me!" he shouts, jumping back.

"Uh-oh," I think. "Turtle-obtuse." Some people can only perceive a few species—terrapins say, or Blandings, or Sulcatas. For others, the obtuseness is complete.

In the booking line downtown, the turtle-less covet the contents of my holster, out of which thick, scaly legs can be seen flailing.

"My tortoise never leaves my side," I tell the cop behind the desk. "Look—see his legs? Go ahead and lift him out."

Pistol an inch from my face, a policewoman gropes my holster with her free hand.

My tortoise voids with a loud "Splooch!"

The policewoman holds her hand out at arm's length. "Shit!" she proclaims.

"That's not a turtle," someone yells.

"All tortoises are turtles," I explain, "though not all turtles are tortoises."

"That's a warthog," the splooched-on cop declares.

Every cop in the station draws down on me.

"Warthogs don't have shells," I insist. "Warthogs are wild African pigs with vicious tusks. The males can top 300 pounds."

"It's a baby," a different cop shouts. "It'll grow."

"It's a California desert tortoise. Ask any herpetologist."

"Now he threatens us with STDs," somebody shrills. "He's a terrorist."

"What's the matter with you people. Are you blind?" I demand, then tack on "No offense," not to pathologize.

WARTHOG PODIATRY

After years of studying how to relieve world hobbling, Warthog stands in a white coat, gnashing his tusks under a blood-red sign: *Warthog Podiatry.*

Will the four wart-like protrusions on his head upset patients? Will he need constantly to explain, "They're great for storing fat, and useful when males fight for females—which happens a lot."

No need, if his patients are warthogs.

The sign, though, muddles things. His name is Warthog, that's for sure. Warthog A. Warthog. But is he the animal, or the jiggly butt of a parental joke about his bad skin and cloven feet? (*Clover feet,* he used to say, and thought them lucky until other kids jeered.)

Did he "go in for" podiatry, as wackos do psychiatry, to heal himself?

What if he's not the doc, but came to *see* a doc who may or may not be a warthog and fix warthog feet?

"One way to find out," he grunts, backing through the office door the way, in Transvaal, he'd back into an abandoned aardvark burrow, ready to burst out in a devastating charge if need be— which, bad feet and all, it often was.

THE NEW MACHINES

Because of problems balloting, the High Court mandates new machines.

Say a man means to vote for Hank Handwringer and his vow to outlaw death, yet inks the oval for Hiram Humperdump, who favors government by entrails of chickens. To be *failsafe*—*foolproof* has been deemed offensive—each machine must record the thought process behind each vote.

To fend off tabulator error, the machines record all tabulators' brain waves, as well as their genomes, since genes determine . . . there's debate; the machines must note that, too.

Our founders limited the vote to adult white male property-owning citizens. Improved ethics widened the circle to adult white male citizens, then to all adult male citizens, then to all adult citizens except felons and "mental defectives."

But felons have opinions. Psychotics may have fascinating ones. The intellectually impaired deserve their say. If they can't say it, we must find out what they mean, and count that, too.

What about children? And the pets we love? And the farm animals who give their all for us. And wild animals, from whom we've taken much.

How about birds? Insects? And plants! Don't slight our vegetable friends.

Other countries should have input. All living things should. Even microbes.

The time required for vote-counting may well exceed the presidential term. In this event, armies will fight, the winning general to be appointed *Acting President*, or for short, *King*. When the King dies, his son will take his place. If he has no son, or a weak one, new armies will fight until all power rests with one man.

Meanwhile, forgotten in some cave, perhaps still counting: the machines.

FYODOR

When I ask for comments on "A Hunger Artist," Fyodor seems stunned, so I ask the student next to him, "How about you?"

She's babbling about "this skinny bone-man hunched behind some straw," when Fyodor gives a grunt, then gags.

"You think Kafka's a buzz-kill, try reading *you*," I say the instant before—with his gaunt face, full black beard, half-a-dozen hairs swept across his scalp's bald tundra—Fyodor drops, thrashing, onto the floor.

The class surrounds him, far enough away to dodge spit or blood, but close enough to see.

I gawk with them until a tall blond boy springs forward. "I'm a lifeguard," he declares.

"Guard his," I say, then, fearing I've been glib, dash for the Dean's.

I burst in screaming, "Help," panting to show sincerity. I can't remember my room number, so the secretary looks it up while I dash back, hoping to head off a lawsuit.

Campus cops are on the scene. "What is your name?" one cop demands. "What is the date?"

Fyodor looks dazed, as if just rescued from a firing squad. "1879," he says.

"What do you mean by *underground man?*" a second cop demands. "Why, if there's no God, is *everything permitted?* Explain *salvation through suffering.*"

Fyodor is led outside, still trying to elucidate.

"Once epileptics were revered," I tell the class—"viewed as shamans who could speak with gods, raise tempests, curse or bless."

My students glare as if I'd jumped under my desk during an earthquake, blubbering. As if terrorists had burst in, and I'd shrieked, "Kill them, not me!"

"Against the backdrop of Fyodor, you stand revealed," the lifeguard jeers.

"Great! Wonderful!" I shout. "What do you see?"

BLADDO

I can do other things now, but I can't do that.
— Bob Dylan

"You poets wouldn't know a rip-off from a slip off a cliff,"
my wife, Annie, declares, and offers a fond sigh as she scoots my
new, reduced-for-quick-sale Bladdo copier into place beside my
Moronique computer.

Bladdo's copy of "Eructations in a Paper Bag" looks fine to
me. But when I read the poem at Lipstick Pipsqueak's open mike,
the ending seems, somehow, improved.

When, as a test, I copy "Dover Beach," what emerges—
"Rover's Leash"—has an irreverent but spiritual wit as far beyond
Matthew Arnold as Victorian gravitas is beyond me. Debuted at
The Faltering Lobster, "Leash" lassos my first Featured Reader
slot.

Bladdo's work (what else to call it?) has charm, charisma, flair.
My stumbling verse, run through Bladdo, comes out ballet. To-do
lists become *bon mots* I drop into chats with Conan, Oprah, Joe
when my memoir, *Average Celery,* tops the *Times* best-seller list.

I quit my job at Jocko's Tacos, buy Annie a Beemer, move us
to Bel Air, send our three kids to dressage school and, at Annie's
urging—"Even great poems don't sell"— start writing novels.

Bladdo's re-vision of *Aunt Scylla's Suspenders* "emulsifies the
tragic and hilarious in a devastating soup," raves uber-critic Harry
"Boom-Boom" Bloom. "The scene where Ming Ling spills her
chowder in *Papa Was a Crustacean* makes Dickens' death of Little
Nell seem like a Tupperware party where everybody buys."

I feel kissed awake by a princess. Fulfilled. Happy, at last, to be
alive.

MR. TWIG

He sprouts, full-blown, from the side of a post oak in Houston, Texas.

He leaves home when Frances Smith—age 9, weight 205—climbs the tree, falls, and besides her arm, breaks him.

He's saved from fungus and slow rot by Cyrus Nutt, a first grade teacher who dresses him in doll clothes and takes him home to Mom.

After a nervous week tucked into Nutt's big bed, Mr. Twig pogos away, and finds work as a bonsai scarecrow. At the Home & Garden Club, he meets a red-haired checker, marries her, and puts down roots into a calm, comfortable life.

"I have problems like anyone," he jokes with friends. "But maintaining a woody isn't one."

He earns his MBA from University of Phoenix, attending class in his spare time.

In games of stickball with his son, he plays the stick, out of pure love.

He buys his wife a black Lab puppy that romps with him around the yard, then drops him, drool-soaked, at the feet of the gardener, who drops him in the trash. After that, he lets his wife deal with José.

She does, too well. DNA tests prove his son has Aztec blood.

Crushed, Mr. Twig moves to Vermont. He likes the fall colors and bonfire-flavored air. He lands a job at the James S. Spickle Spackle Company, and re-marries: a thin lecturer from the local JC.

Watching their daughter smash fallen maple leaves, he tells her, "Kiss your cousins. Each is a departed piece of shade."

He tells his boss, "December light sifts like blue-gray talcum from the sky."

"What you been smokin', Twig?" his boss replies.

Mr. Twig dreams of being a human boy. He sees Dad jumping waves with him at Galveston, Mom in her rocker reading him *The Barbary Pirates* as he swims, gasping, up from flu's delirium.

He wakes with his head stuck to his pillow by sap that leaks from the two worm-holes he's learned it's best to call his *eyes*.

FAMILIARITY

"You're better than Prince Charming," she said when they first kissed. "Strong, handsome, fast, bullet-proof, able to fly—like a combination boyfriend / fighter jet."

Friends tell him, "Maintain your mystique. Keep her distant, guessing, hanging on." But on his home planet, Krypton, familiarity bred respect and deeper love. So he took her to his Fortress of Solitude, and let her see him in skivvies, and on the pot.

Soon she was mocking his furniture, griping that he left socks on the floor, and when he had an early rescue, "banged around" while she was trying to sleep. He was "stubborn, conceited, chauvinistic."

"Who," she demanded, "do you think you are?"

When he told her, she said, "Another thing: you're arrogant!"

She still liked sex; he was, after all, a man of steel. Sometimes, though, she'd lie there between orgasms with a "When will it end?" stare.

His powers were a problem, too. They made her feel "less than." They fostered "marital inequity." Half of them, she stated, were legally hers.

On Krypton, "Till death do us part" meant what it said. When she complained for the millionth time, "We never go out anymore," he said, "How's this?" and scooped her up the way he did on their first dates.

"Ow," she yelped. "Don't be so rough."

"Sorry," he said. Then—Metropolis twinkling below as she explained, "This is okay, but it's what *you* like to do"—his heart-of-steel breaking, he let her go.

WHAT WOULD FREUD DO?

The counselor's closet contains two bataca sticks, four cushions for group work, a yellowed copy of *I'm Okay, You're Okay*, but no trace of the clothes that vanished off her body five minutes before.

Beneath her twin leather chairs, she finds only two quarters, a dime, and enough dust to sack the cleaning lady, which she will this time, she swears—show that assertiveness she touts!

But first things first. The waiting room she shares with three other psychotherapists is littered with notices from the Psych Board encouraging patients to sue. Ask her fellow shrinks to lend her clothes, and they'll report her "inappropriate attire." Psychotherapy is long on Ethics, short on cures.

She could ignore the flashing red light that announces *him*. But how can she call herself Doctor, cowering in this room while the person in the world who most admires, needs, maybe even loves her, writhes in pain?

"Wait," she tells herself. "Who's the mind-expert here?"

She can say, "Naked? In what way?"

She can suggest he has undressed her with his eyes. Or claim *projection*: insist *he* is the naked one.

She can say, "Here, put these on," holding out her empty hands.

SECRETS OF THE BODY, REVEALED

While people sleep, their toes pop out of foot-holes and hop into the streets where, meeting other toes, they hold revels of which nice people do not speak. A psychic hook-up with their hosts helps to conceal their wanderings. Blinding speed helps, too. Still, people who leap from bed frequently fall.

Lovers may wake with toes on one another's feet. Or two toes may claim the same hole. Roused by the fight, the foot's owner tells himself, "just a bad dream."

The fingers—solemn, pious—roam infrequently, but lacking the toes' speed and homing sense, create more woes. When they jam into toe holes, the owner may strain his back scratching his nose.

A nose-and-penis switch exemplifies *obscene.*

Arms and legs, too, enjoy a midnight stroll. Knowledgeable burglars lock all doors of a house, then take what they please while owners flip like flounders in their beds.

To thwart such fiends, I own no valuables.

To stop the monstrous practice of foot-piping, I sleep in metal shoes with doggie-doors large enough to let toes come and go, but small enough to ward off all lips but the wind's.

THE GOLD STANDARD

In ancient times, blackberries were free: sweet blisters, warm in summer sun. But people over-plucked. To get blackberries then, you had to trade gold, or if not gold, something priced in terms of gold, because people valued gold—women because they thought it made them beautiful; men because it bought power and beautiful wives.

"The Gold Standard means I require so much gold per year," my wife says, teasing. Or is she?—gold earrings in both ears, gold rings, bracelets, and necklaces, gold barrettes in auburn hair, a golden tan under a clingy blue silk dress threaded with gold.

Ideal of alchemists, gold won't tarnish or rust, won't dissolve in anything except a mix of acids called *aqua regia*, "water of kings."

Aztecs called gold, *sweat of the sun*. Cortez told Montezuma, "We Spaniards have a heart-disease that only gold can cure."

If the world had roared, "Gold schmold—give us cow pies," Tenochtitlan might have survived. Instead, countries printed bills redeemable for gold, but safer, gold being so soft that it rubs off on hands, diminishing the world's wealth day by day.

Soon, countries outlawed private ownership of gold. "We'll keep your gold for you," officials said, thinking, "Since you'll take paper, we'll print lots of it."

But with more money in the world, people charged more for berries. And wanted it in gold.

"Our paper is as good as gold," officials decreed. "Don't make us hurt you."

The Fear Standard was born.

Inflation sprang out of its bottle—snarling, not perky and compliant like gold-haired Barbara Eden in *I Dream of Genie*, who made men think, "If I owned her, I know what *I'd* command. Right after *Bring me lots of gold*."

Panics dropped like cyclones from the sunless sky. Millions lost jobs and/or committed suicide. Ex-tycoons wore barrels and sang, "Brother, can you spare me a Troy ounce?" until—slowly, as Joe Citizen leaned into his pump—prosperity's gold elixir bubbled back.

Even today, when wealth is stored in data banks, miners still squirm through stinking pits to claw out baskets of black mud that hide potential bracelets, earrings, wedding bands. People kill for a chance to wash the miners' hands. They love Lady Gold the way I love my wife, and coat myself in filth for her.

Millions world-wide still hoard gold. Jeremiahs still shriek "Doom!" and beg their countries to revive the Gold Standard. Meanwhile, the economy—including my bank account, retirement funds, chance to buy a new house and a bass boat, to have children and educate them well while meeting my wife's gold standard—it all chugs forward like that cartoon coyote who runs off a cliff above a snarl of blackberry vines, and can keep running as long as he doesn't look down.

CHANGING ROOM

"Can you direct me to the Changing Room?" Thutmose asks a salesclerk who's folding blouses under a cloud of teased red hair.

"That's hard to do," she says. "It keeps changing."

Thut pinches off an inch of smile. Loaded with clothes he hopes will lift him above the rank of Default Bashee in the world's Drubbing Order, he's in no mood for jokes. "I'm serious," he says. "I need to change."

"Look around until you see the sign," the sales clerk says. "You might find something else you like."

A sales ploy, sure. Still, her trained eye must judge the duds he picked so carefully as duds indeed.

"It *was* behind the sports bras," offers one of four boyish-looking men dressed, cave-man style, in animal skins. "It keeps moving, in case of predators."

"What would eat a Changing Room?" Thut demands.

"A Changingroom-asaurus," one of the four shoots back.

"A Changingroom-ophagus," another quips.

"We started off as the Four Lads," a third explains. "Then we changed to the Four Freshmen, Four Aces, Four Seasons, Four Tops, Four Preps, Four Perps. Gold records every time. Now"—he indicates his clothes—"we're the Four Skins."

The quartet produce four guffaws.

Thut wants to huff out of the store. But celebrities keep walking by. Elvis in his jumpsuit. Marilyn with her curves. Einstein with his atomic hair.

A bearded man in dusty robes approaches, leading a pregnant woman on a spavined ass.

Just past Maternity, the air shimmers and glows.

Shifting his heavy clothes-stack arm to arm, Thutmose rushes toward the light.

JURY DUTY

On my right side, a woman is writing *The Mom's Book of Pantoums.* On my left, a mechanic (his shirt says Francis Hung) reads *Himmler's Hingeback: A Novel of Turtles in the Third Reich.*

A judge dressed in undertaker-black clomps in to say, over a sputtering P.A., that juries are either "the grease that keeps this nation running smooth," or "the slop that stops us up."

"Moms love a good pantoum," the poet says. "It's a market niche I mean to fill."

"Remember those little green turtles Woolworth's sold for a dime?" Francis Hung says. "We put them in a plastic island-thing with half an inch of brown water that smelled like poo, and fed them ant eggs till their shells went soft and Mom flushed them with no funeral or adieu."

"Red-ear sliders," I say. "*Trachemys scripta elegans.*"

Voices ring out of the jury pool. "Mine died too." "They were so cute." "Poor little Swimmy. I cried for a month."

"My sister raised hers in a fish aquarium, and fed them hamburger," I say. "When they got too big, she'd drive them to Skeets Lake. They looked puzzled when she set them on the shore. Their heads swung back and forth. Then they'd dash into the lake, and swim away like they'd been freed in paradise."

Francis Hung begins to sob. "I didn't know. . ."

"You were a kid," the bailiff says. "What do kids know?"

"A good mom knows her pantoums," our bard asides as Hung pulls his head into his coat.

Lunch hour passes with no evidence of lunch. I wonder: will my case be criminal or civil? Claiming descent from sea monkeys? Transporting dentures across state lines?

"My better judgment has decayed from lack of practice," someone wails.

"*Fudge Not Lest Ye Be Fudged*! That's my next pantoum," the poet confides.

"Two hundred million years of thriving, then extinct in the next hundred. What's the punishment for that?" cries Francis Hung, stroking the green-and-yellow-striped neck of his tie.

EGG SALAD DAYS

Except ye see signs and wonders, ye will not believe.
— John 4:48

We gorged on the clouds' bounty that first day, and blessed our luck: not too much mayo, just chunky enough. Slapped on a slice of Trader Joe's sprouted rye, this modern manna beat Nate 'n Al's to a thin slush.

When I complained, "It wrecks my shoes," Katie replied, "People are starving. Or haven't you heard?"

"How can I, with egg salad in my ears?"

"Don't exaggerate," she said. "It'll stop soon."

She's not so bloody sanguine now. The stuff's seeped into our crawl-space. It threatens to occupy our living room and spoil two thousand dollars worth of Oak Barrel carpeting.

The hill behind us is heaped high. One little earthquake, and we're toast.

The news is full of downed trees, power outages, and fatal wrecks. Traffic is mired, San Diego to José.

The pump I bought at Home Despot can't keep up with what rains down. As I lug buckets to the street, the landscape looks like yellow tundra with white boulders and a little celery. Drains are clogged; sky, the greenish-yellow of a hard-boiled yolk.

My neighbors' yards are as bad as mine—all but Reverend Grebe's. He drags out his Christmas creche in mid-July. Barbecue grill hissing, he lifts charcoaled brisket to the sky as Handel's *Messiah* blares.

Aside from a pine needle-glaze, his yard's pristine. Even the sky over his head is baby blue.

"It's so unfair," I observe.

"I may rejoin the church," Katie confides.

IN THE HALL OF WASTED QUESADILLAS

The first one failed to please—its tortilla too old; the cheese only Cheese Whiz with, the boy declared, "a throw-up stench."

The next was better—fresh tortilla; melted cheddar, warm and gold. The boy opened his mouth just as the doorbell called him to baseball.

The third was excellent, but following two others just as good, went in the trash—beneath spoiled shrimp chow mein, so Dad wouldn't see.

The fourth was ruined when the cat walked on it—the boy willing to eat it; Mom not willing to let him.

The fifth contained, instead of cheese, a paste of "stink-bugs, worms, and doggy-doo," his sister said.

"Liar," he yelled. And left it on his plate.

We move, next, to the Hall of Wasted Milk: frozen into cow-shapes; soaked with useless tears.

From there, it's a short walk to the Hall of Wasted Vegetables, which—arranged by shape and color, then sealed into baggies with snapshots of starving kids—infect with guilt the carefree childhood years.

HALF IN LOVE WITH EASEFUL DEATH

He had sexy hair, black as Tiffany's cat Sin (for Singularity), accentuated by tomato-lips and cream-cheese skin.

"He looks like Dracula," Tiffy's best friend Pammi said.

"His name's Kevin," Tiffy explained.

"I wouldn't cut your finger near him," Pammi said. "Or let him give you a hickey."

Going on dates in his hearse creeped Tiffy out. But her mom loved the white lilies he brought to every meal. She collected his thank-you notes in Gothic script.

"The man has manners," she said. "And a distinguished hand."

"He does," Tiffy said, then blushed so hard that she felt slapped. After *le petit mort*, she would lie in his arms and sleep like the . . . whatever.

In all her nineteen years, she'd never felt so free. Still, she panicked at, "Will you marry me?"

"Is my job the problem?" he said. "The scythe's a pain, you don't have to tell me. Try getting on an elevator. Or catching a cab. Airports are hell. And the hours—worse than ob-gyns'. I'm looking into other work. The military. Or the FDA."

"Lawyers make good money," she said.

"*Kevin Grimm, Esquire.* Does have a nice ring," he said, and slipped a big one on her wilting hand.

LOCH NESS MOBSTER

After forty frittered years, Randolph "Randy" Ness, great-great-grand-nephew of Eliot Untouchable, tells his wife, "It's my last chance to make a splash," and heads for the family Loch.

Lugging his mobster hat and suit, his fat mobster cigar, his Tommy-Gun-in-a-viola-case, he rents a room at The Grouse & Trout, then, when fog cloaks him in mystery, stomps pub to pub, booming "Hi, I'm *Dutch*," and thrusting out his hand.

"Poor Yank's off his nut," the locals think, but ask politely about Amsterdam.

When, over breakfast, he meets a *Discovery Channel* camera crew, he climbs into costume, and treks to the loch.

"Back!" barks Security. "We're trying to film a monster here."

"Mobster, you idiots," Randy thinks. Hoping they'll realize their mistake, he strikes mobster-poses on the rocky shore, staring into peat-dark depths as moss-green highlands lour.

"Anything could hide down there," he thinks, and doesn't see what's surfacing off-shore: icepick teeth masked by mist, boat-long tail fanning the waves already snapping at his feet.

REALISTS

"My protagonists are three teenage girls," Zoey states. "They hang out at the mall and text their friends and flirt with boys and experiment with makeup and making out. In bed at night, they fret about grades and college and who'll take them to the prom and how many kids they'll have. The best part is, they're unicorns."

In the silence that ensues, Hermes pulls his socks over his ankle-wings. "How do they text with hooves?" he says.

"How do they get their prom-dresses over their horns?" Woden wonders, adjusting his eye-patch.

Zoey looks like she's been gored by Minotaur.

Horus, our workshop leader, smooths his feathered hair and scratches his hawk-nose. "I assume it's a kid's book?"

"I didn't think . . . I just . . . excuse me," Zoey gasps, and runs, blubbering, out of the room.

It would be poignant, in a French-cinematic way, if once she's gone, we realize that all of us have forehead-horns. Or maybe we see the voids where, in a better world, our horns would be.

Alas, all of us are realists.

"Were we too hard on her?" Aphrodite asks when, after five minutes, Zoey hasn't returned.

"A writer needs thick skin," Basilisk says.

"You're quiet, 'Dusa," Anubis tells me, a French beret balanced on his jackal-ears. "What do you think?"

"Mythic creatures in the normal world are an exhausted trope," I say, and squelch the urge to snap, "Stop hissing!" at my hair.

INSTANT BABY

A single box costs six months' salary, but the couple buys.

She doesn't want the morning sickness, the stretch marks, the pregnant waddle. He doesn't want her breasts to sag, hips to widen, vagina to stretch.

Because the box says BOY, they buy blue baby clothes, and paint the room "cerulean."

They diaper the box, place it in a hand-made walnut crib, and baby-talk to it, predicting it will be a great musician / neurosurgeon / shortstop / President. They play the box Mozart and Bach. They tell it bedtime stories: *The Velveteen Rabbit. Pinocchio.* Still, they put off mixing it until the woman passes menopause and says, "I think it's time."

"His presence will complete our lives," her husband says.

A CD called "Sweet Dreams" soothes their nerves as they empty their box into a bowl, then add one quart warm water to the peach-colored mix.

A baby takes shape in the bowl. He has his dad's broad shoulders, his mom's aqua eyes.

"Pick him up," the man whispers. "He wants mommy."

The baby squalls, and in an instant, with a match-sized flash and mouse-sized poof of lilac dust, is gone.

COLLEGE OF BABIES

Did you think babies squeeze out of the womb knowing how to ululate and foul their diapers, much less babble, coo, and shriek all night?

Of course they don't. They come here to learn.

Nobody wants to see a newborn kip up, towel dry, stretch, and articulate, "How 'bout a blanket, Doc, before I freeze my keister?"

First word, first smile, first step, all gone bye-bye? Who would stand for that?

The rare times that a baby calls for the potty right away, writes with crayon and butcher paper, "Barney sucks," or simply fails to fuss or babble, people freak.

"Ignorant egghead," they rage. "Stupid fuckin' genius!"

A JEALOUS DAD

dumps his son out of his crib, and climbs inside. Now when he feels sad, his wife coos, "Mommy's little love," and pops a nipple in his mouth.

What delight to let go when the urge strikes, then lie back babbling "Ga!" and "Goo!" while his wife changes his dydee and gives him a warm bath. What satisfaction to be carried everywhere.

He loves how Winnie the Pooh floats above his head. He loves to watch the constellations—Piglet, Tigger, Eore—spin.

He worships at his crib's mirror every day.

Let his son drive the lump of ignominy Detroit calls a "Striver," looking forward to a stiff Scotch and limp sit-coms after a hard day. Let his son's belt-size expand every spine-crushing year. Let his son pay an arm and a leg for dismemberment insurance, and lug home the bacon that will clog his heart and stop it cold one day.

"HANDSOME CAN SIT UP BY HIMSELF,"

Erik declares, holding Grandma's gift: a plush new teddy bear.

"Fev can do that," answers Dad who, the day Erik was born, bought him a teddy bear named Fev, just like the one *he* had.

Fev's fur is coarser than Handsome's. He has stump-legs and, lying on his back—all he's really built to do—looks more like a hairy gingerbread man than a bear.

"Fev's legs don't bend," Erik says. "He can't sit up."

"Neither can Hamstrung," Dad says.

"Yes he can!" Erik sits Handsome on his bed. "His name's Handsome."

The bear's ample rear is made for sitting. His back legs bend exactly right. His well-formed front feet, spread to offer bear-hugs, add stability—until Dad shoves him down.

"Fev sits better than that," Dad says. (His wife calls Fev "that sad old thing.")

"You knocked him down," Erik objects.

"Poor Hamster lost his balance," Dad says.

Erik sits the bear back up. "His name's Handsome."

Erik has seen Monty Python, but doesn't grasp, at not-quite-four, the finer points of Silliness. Still, Dad shoves Handsome down again, then sits on his own hands.

"You pushed him," Erik says. "Tell the truth!"

That stops Dad cold. Instead of God, their family venerates Truth.

"I might've bumped him," Dad admits.

He slept with his Fev every night, rubbing him against his nose until there was a slick, shiny, bare *nose-place* on Fev's face. Erik's Fev has the start of a nose-place.

When Erik sets Handsome down out of Dad's reach, Dad says, "Hambone may not be sitting on his own. Maybe it's magic."

"His name's Handsome," Erik says. "Tell the truth."

"It's hard, sometimes, to know what's true," Dad says.

"There's no such thing as magic," Erik states. "Ms Nune said."

Ms Nune is his pre-school teacher: a Russian-Armenian with, Dad can see, a classically materialist point of view.

The truth is, Handsome *is* handsome: a Kodiak, most likely, his fur thick, brown and sleek as if he's spent weeks yanking salmon from clear, rushing streams, stuffing his handsome face with them, as well as wild berries and honey, then washing in the river's cold gush, letting the sun dry him as it sizzles down on the glorious Arctic summer that's over almost before it begins.

II

THE ELEPHANT OF SURPRISE

The rooster of arrogance struts through the barnyard, cock-a-doodle-doodling for all to hear.

The antelope of enthusiasm leads the parade, rhinestoned antlers glittering.

The guinea pigs of chagrin carpet the carpet, glad to trip you up and knock you down.

The puppy of embarrassment humps your leg no matter where you hide.

The elephant of surprise, though, glides stealthy as a snake; flies silent as an owl; stalks noiseless as a panther before— trumpeting loudly enough to kill the living, then wake them up again—it springs.

THE SKY RAINS BLOOD
— For H.P.

"Airplanes have scalpeled its blue skin," someone yells. "Bandage it in clouds before it dies!"

"The air has breathed mustard gas and is hemorrhaging," someone warns. "Styptic pencil rockets are our only hope."

"The sky's a woman," someone snaps. "Shut your eyes. Give her some privacy."

"God has a nosebleed," someone testifies. "If He lies down and puts His head back, He'll be fine."

"Not one god—gods!" someone proclaims. "They've sacrificed a constellation. Bigger gods are angry. There'll be hell to pay."

Rivers flow red to viscous seas. The moon, a glowing cherry cough-drop, soars.

The temperature dives. Lacey, geometric scabs drift down.

A WORKING-CLASS GYRO

I'm right behind him in the cafeteria line. Full beard, granny glasses, shoulder-length brown hair with *Abbey Road*-style all-white shirt, coat, pants, and shoes, he picks the Dinkum Dog. I go with Humbo Jumbo Pie.

He squints at his "side" of slaw—"What's this, then?"—as he slides into the crowd, me close behind.

Two empty seats appear: kid-sized, but we sit down.

"Haddy Grimble, Randoob," I say, to let him know I know.

"Musty Chrustchove, old pal buddy," he replies.

I mumble, "How's Yoko?" If he takes offense, I'll claim I said, "How's go-go?" This seems a good plan at the time.

"Nobody's shot her. What more can you arsk?" he says, and laughs to let me know it's all okay.

"Any new songs in the works?"

Grinding his Dinkum Dog, he nods. "One called 'A Working Class Gyro.' Or 'Nero' or 'Zero.' *It's among me best*," he says, the way he said, *The people in the cheap seats clap your hands. The rest of you, rattle your jewelry.*

The PA blasts "Ticket to Die," played on kazoos.

"I tried to buy that tape and bloody burn it," he says. "The publisher hung on like a case o' crabs."

The *u* in *publisher* sounds like the *u* in *pudding*. I want to tell him how I imitated this to seem British, which my dad's parents were. I want to say that my first band, The Super Sports, never mastered the "She Loves You" harmonies, and that the only words I ever spoke to heart-shredding Keri Kronenberg were, "Did you see the Beatles on TV?"

I want to ask what happened between him and Paul, and tell him how, when my friend Jon and I stopped talking, it was like a marriage down in flames. I want to tell my dream where I tire-tooled Mark David Chapman's head, screaming, "*Imagine*'s the greatest song I know," and the crazy bastard grinned.

I need to keep things light, though: two average blokes, grabbing a bite.

"What's lobscouse like?" I say to show I know my Liverpool.

"Nothin' to write a gnome about," he quips as "Iron the Waldorf" blasts from the P.A.

I grope for something insightful to say: "I love the way you dressed your Genghis Khan as Gandhi"? "A good song is a virus that turns dumping-by-Trudi into making-out-with-Pam"?

Instead I say, "Nobody blames you for British Petroleum."

"One sea turtle's worth a million crapitalists," he says.

NO GRAMPAS HERE

In the short run, virgin birth works well for *Lepidodactylus lugubris.* These Pacific-island geckos—all females—maintain their genetic advantage by self-cloning, never mixing genes. When the environment changes, though, *lugubris*—unable to adapt—will die.

Rather than waste energy leaving its cave on stormy days when few insects are in the air, the eastern pipistrelle reads barometric pressure with its "Vitalis organ," which also keeps its fur shiny and sleek.

Fish-jaws evolved from gill arches, which soon required gill-arch-supports.

Detergents work when *surfacants*—long molecules with heads that love water, and tails that hate it—cling to submerged dirt, the tails fighting to surface; the heads, to dive. Their jostling disturbs the dirt which, loosening its bite to complain, is washed away.

Global warming could lead to bad poetry on a large scale if malaria mosquitoes migrate north, bringing their "First whine, best whine" philosophy.

Aging male baboons will leave their troop, dye their fur with berry juice, brave the dangers of the wild and a new troop—anything not to be called "Gramps."

HEART OF HEARTS

An air-mattress decides that, in its heart of hearts, it is a set of shepherd's pipes. But no one plays it. And like a wife too proud to mention that her husband won't kiss her, it doesn't speak.

"When will you offer me support like you're supposed to?" it's fat-slob owner wails.

The air-mattress keeps mum.

"Each time I see a pretty girl and charge into the surf to frolic with her, you sink like a bathyscaphe," the owner bleats.

Still the air mattress keeps mum.

"Your dereliction drags my status down, and dulls the luster of my sexual approach," the owner whines. "You trifling lollygagger, why don't you float?"

"Why don't you play?" the mattress wheezes.

"Great. A leak," the owner keens. "That's all I need."

Throwing the mattress down, he stomps on it until he's panting, then kicks it out into the waves. "You're no damn good to me," he sobs.

"Or me," the surf spits, tossing the mattress back on land.

"Or me," the sand hisses, blasting the mattress, then piling on top of it.

All that remains is a slight bulge on the beach when, just at dusk, a squall roars up, sunset's gold-and-purple robe flapping behind.

"Everyone stand back!" howls the wind which, having decided in its heart of hearts that it's a shepherd, whisks the sand away, picks up the mattress, and collecting its cloud-sheep, begins to play.

IVY-COVERED MONKEY

For her judge-father's sixtieth, Traci buys, from an artisan friend, a wire monkey covered in ivy.

"Thanks, Sweetheart," he says, and gives her gift a place of honor by the amethyst impatiens. But it spoils the redwood deck he built himself, where he likes to rest after a hard day's sentencing. It's like a stain on the floor he can't scrub out, a clogged sprinkler he is enjoined not to fix.

An ivy-covered squirrel might be okay. A tortoise, maybe, or even a gnome—anything but a hairy, quasi-man, tail raised to fart, hand cocked to fling feces.

The judge wastes two weekends searching for where Traci bought the thing. Exchange impossible, he condemns it to die—not consciously, of course; he under-waters until its leaves wilt and fall, leaving a wire corpse that he soaks twice a day to prove he tried.

"I'll have it replanted," Traci says when she stops by.

The very day the thing returns, the judge finds a deep scratch on his new Lexus. *That's about as welcome as an ivy-covered monkey,* he thinks, and has to smile.

The next day, he warns a glib shyster, "Don't ivy-covered monkey me!"

Through the mind-numbing trial of a twice-paroled rapist who burned a woman and her kids alive, he pictures the monkey in the jury box, unmoved by the man's good looks and disadvantaged youth. The monkey's curved tail brings to mind a water-park where the judge played as a boy, and his one take-away from three years of piano: the word *glissando,* from the French *glisser,* "to slide."

KINDNESS DETECTOR

It looks like a bamboo flute, but has a motor that draws air across a copper plate treated with chemicals which, exposed to empathy, the urge to serve, concern for others, and the like, make the flute toot "When the Saints Go Marching In."

Once detected, the exceptionally kind are followed to their homes and forcibly enrolled at the Institute for General Decency. Novices practice dropping coins in beggars' hands, helping strangers who fall in the street, smiling non-sexually at passers-by, and giving small gifts—a plush kitten, a sudoku game—for no reason at all.

Intermediates learn to let a driver cut into a crush of cars and not *aoogah* when *that* driver lets someone else in.

Advanced students spend hours climbing trees to free stuck kites for kids, and never file a lawsuit when they fall.

In this way, we cull our culture's saboteurs, and keep them busy, amid fragrant flowers and trees, where the good they do does little harm at all.

DINNER WITH THE BLITHERVILLES

Chez Blitherville looked like Chez Lamborghini when I arrived. Valets scampered about in hats and tails while, from the house—built like a larger Versailles—came clinks and clunks, bells and yells, cries and sighs of revelry.

I'd bought new clothes so I'd look sharp, and memorized *Principia Mathematica* so I'd have smart things to say. I'd gone to Arthur Murray daily for a week, in case Colonel B should drawl, after dessert, "Let's to the ballroom, and shake our many legs." Colonel B's no square. Or Mrs. B, if half the gossip is half true.

"I've made my *Salmon Coppertone* for you—not seared, just slightly sunburned," she might say when I walked in, voice undulant and smooth. Then, pulling me into a closet big as Dodger Stadium, she'd part her lips . . .

I wiped sweat from my face, clumped up the marble stairs, and banged on the bronze door.

A butler dressed as Louis Quatorze scanned my invitation, then his list of guests. "Pardon," he says, "but your dinner for next week rescheduled is."

I squelched a scream, and chirped, with all the good cheer I could fake, "Then I'll see your Supreme Sun-Kingship then."

Pius XII, or his facsimile, rushed forward. "Oh Loo-*eee*!" he told the butler, and looked as if I were the punch-line of a *très déclassé* joke. "Monsieur Dwindlebaum was our guest last night. Regrettably, no one may dine here twice."

"An imposter," I huffed. "Obviously."

"Who would dare impersonate *you?*" the pontiff soothed, unction staining his immaculate white robes.

Memory flicked back ON. What about "Get out and stay out!" did I not understand?

"Tell Mrs. B—Eulalia—something romantic," I said, and tumbled backwards down the stairs.

I LOVE HER SO MADLY,

want so much to please, that when she complains that I leave dandruff on the sheets, whiskers in the sink, pee on the toilet seat, I build a large black plastic cube to live inside.

Five pin-sized air-holes and a straw through which I sip protein drinks are my sole contact with the world in which my dear one shines.

I've learned to re-absorb my wastes, and will my beard back into my face. Since, in the darkness of my cube, the sweat that lacquers my underarms can't gleam, and lost hairs flutter, soft as feathers, to the unseen floor, I no longer fear offending.

Still, the groans and whimpers wafting from our bed, the clink of male belts, and an intermittent scraping makes me fear that, even now, my box is edging out the door.

SURPRISE

One week to the day after he aced his yearly physical, JJ Bunn is climbing out of his Toyota Prius when his heart loses its place in the score it has played perfectly for fifty-seven years. Next thing he knows, two doctors—bare-chested, in white papyrus pants—are bending over him.

One is tall, with mad-scientist eyes. The other—fleshy, with the soft gaze of a priest—shoves a metal hook up JJ's sinuses, then flails the hook like an egg-scrambler until whipped brain froths out his nose.

The doctors swab out JJ's skull with linen strips, then pack it tight with linen rubbed in frankincense. They slit him open with a black obsidian knife, slop his organs into jars, and pack the torso with white dust they call *natron*. Then they bury him under the stuff.

For thirty days, he floats above his body, peaceful as he'd hoped to be on that Buddhist retreat which he spent sweating a botched order for brake shoes. When the doctors return, JJ is brown-black as jerky, and weighs seventy-nine pounds. Seventy-seven pounds of water have seeped into the natron, which now smells like wet sand.

The doctors rub JJ's skin with linen soaked in oil containing frankincense, myrrh, cedar, lotus, and palm wine. They individually wrap his fingers, toes, arms, legs, and penis in linen painted with heiroglyphs, then wrap his whole body in linen strips fastened with cedar-sap.

Mad Scientist chants tongue-contorting words which JJ understands to mean, "O doubly powerful, eternally young and mighty Mistress of the East and Lady of the West, may breath return to this man's chest."

Next thing JJ knows, he's standing by a gin-clear stream

where, copper skin gleaming, naked girls giggle and splash.

"These must be angels," JJ thinks.

A man with a jackal's head leaps from behind a sand dune, and trots his way.

"Ramses!" the jackal-man yips. "Four thousand years no see!"

PHARAOH THANKS GOD FOR THE EXODUS

When Aaron hurled down his staff and it became a snake, I'd have given him and his addle-pated brother Moses anything they asked—until my priests turned their own staves into snakes.

When Aaron's snakes ate theirs, my priests said, "We could do that. But we're out of staves."

When Aaron smote the Nile and turned it into blood, I would have led his people out of Egypt personally. My priests, though, insisted, "Wait," then when the water cleared, turned it to blood again.

When Moses, muttering and drooling, caused frogs to slime the Queen's makeup, and a big one popped out of my lunch, I thought "Enough!" But my priests cast their own spells, and brought more frogs. So, though the palace was knee-deep in amphibians, I kept my Hebrews. Frog legs are a delicacy. And my favorite daughter loved "cute hoppy-toads."

The gnats weren't cute, or conjurable by my priests. "Behold," they said, "the Hebrews do abominations, and smell worse than their goats. Let's let them go."

That's when I went a little mad. Because the gnats didn't convince me. Or the flies. Or the plague on our livestock.

The queen barred me from her bed for my "accursed hard-headedness." Not that I wanted sex, with both of us covered in boils.

When the Hebrews' god, Yahweh, killed every Egyptian first-born, including my own son, I summoned my army at last, and drove the dung-breathed herd-humpers into the sea.

Yahweh parted it for them, then—sploosh!—smashed it down on my army. Yet today, I honor Him. Our gods had grown soft, caring more for poems, statues, and "human rights" than for the noble art of war. They were no match for snarling, sweaty Yahweh—as lean and merciless as those who served him. As in love with burning flesh.

Egypt regained its greatness under me, and kept it for a thousand years. I praise Yahweh for showing me how cruel, to get His will done, a loving God must be.

REPLACEMENT PEOPLE

The real people go on strike for higher salaries and more control of their own destiny.

The gods, who loved putting people through their paces, cheering and jeering as they scrambled, sweated, flailed, offer their jobs to animals.

The animals reject the offer. Higher consciousness is too much to pay.

The plants hiss, "Not on your life!" They much prefer to stand in one place, feasting on sunshine and air.

Rocks reject the gods' offer with that silence called "stony."

Finally, the gods ask man-made things: coffee pots and chairs, automobiles and nose-hair clippers, skateboards and didgeridoos. These, having long envied their masters, seize their chance.

At first, they bungle things. A table scuffling to school gets crushed by a runaway bus. A feather boa can't hit a ball out of the infield. A Ming vase and a red clay flowerpot fight for the same pedestal, and smash to shards on the wriggling concrete floor.

Gradually, though, skill-levels rise until even the most demanding gods are satisfied. When the real people—aging, bored—beg to return to work, the gods reply, "Knock yourselves out." But they no longer hear the prayers of their once-favorite creations, or notice if they live or as they die.

DEPARTMENT OF DISCONTENT

The officer in charge checks my ID, and asks, "Formal or informal complaint?"

When I hesitate, she says, "Informal's more relaxed. You speak more softly, don't raise your blood pressure, can wear jeans, no tie, use contractions and slang. Very *chill*, as the kids say. With formal complaints, you have to shout. Formal complainants sometimes die of strokes. Also, you need to wear a tux."

"Which one works better?"

"That's confidential. Either way, we interview everyone in your complaint, then everyone in those interviews, everyone in those, etcetera. *Leave no tern un-stoned*, as the joke goes."

"When will I know the results?"

"You won't. They're confidential, too."

"How does that help me?"

"Well," she observes, "you already look younger than your I.D. Less beaten-down."

"I *did* get energized, thinking I'd stand up for myself."

"And so you have. Complainants sleep better, having *taken steps*. They walk taller for having had their say. Never doubt that, out there in the Dark Beyond, Justice sends a big, wet kiss your way."

A SITUATION OF EXTREME HOPELESSNESS

A drifter who wants a swim jumps, naked, off a bridge, and finds himself suspended in mid-air.

Turns out the river won't have him. It's sick and tired of human filth. The drifter hasn't bathed in weeks, and has open genital sores.

"We can't have infected wee-wees waggling above our town," the mayor declares. "Ladies' book clubs are meeting. Kids are on their way to school."

Overnight, the man is changed from just another bum into a textbook refutation of Free Will. The Chamber of Commerce gives him twelve hours to "clean up your act, or be blasted out of the blue."

The evening news calls his "a situation of extreme hopelessness." He must not only heal his sores and call down a rain mixed with soap and shampoo; he must pull clean clothes out of the soot-choked sky.

MANDARIN PALACE OF DOOM

"Let's see what Confucius says," I tell Ahab, crack my cookie's sugary puffin-beak, and read, *"Anteaters will feast on your spleen."*

The words are out before I realize that speaking them might make them stick.

"Don't look so glum, Hamlet," Anna K tells me, and downs a lychee. "Last week my fortune said, *Faberge eggs will crush your skull.* And look—I'm fine."

"For now," Count Vronsky says.

"I got one that said *You'll die in agony, guts eaten out by cancer,*" Huck says. "They gave me a new one."

"Which said what?" Romeo demands.

"Nice try, Blood-In-Your-Stool," Huck says.

Gatsby scoffs. "What kind of dimwit takes those fortunes seriously?"

"I refuse to open mine," Pandora says.

"Brilliant," Sisyphus chides. "Shut your eyes, and slam into a giant rock."

"Anteaters aren't common in LA. I can avoid them," I attest.

"No trips to South America," Ishmael warns.

"Or Central," Hester adds.

"Right," I say. "And no zoos. I hate to see imprisoned creatures anyway."

"Watch out for people named Anteater," Hulga says.

"No one's named Anteater," I say.

"Foreign names can mean strange things," Smerdyakov says.

"A girl I knew married a man named Pogroszewski," Desdemona states. "It meant *Cabbage Gives Me Gas.* Something like that."

"Don't date anyone who lists *Exotic Pets* under *Interests,*" Emma suggests.

"I loathe dating," Gertrude protests. Too much?

"Trying to dodge bad luck makes you walk into it," Pip says. "Just look at Oedipus."

"Calm down, my queen," he tells his phone. "What's Ancestry-dot-com?"

"MAN TRIES TO BLOW UP MUSEUM OF TOLERANCE"

— The Los Angeles Times

"I can't stand her," 9-year-old Doc wails after Jane bloodies his nose and steals his Nolan Ryan hat.

"It's not nice not to stand people," Mom says, and keeps watering her weeds.

When Doc calls lima beans "yucky green purses stuffed with dirt," Mom says, "Sshh! Daddy works hard for every bean."

"Quit your job," Doc tells Daddy, who wears earplugs for tranquility, and a sweatshirt that proclaims PROUD MEMBER OF THE CLEAN PLATE CLAN.

Piano lessons, Sunday school, visiting Aunt Sepia in the Old Folks Home—so many things that Doc can't stand, especially compared to baseball, bonfires, watermelon and Carly Swenson's golden hair.

"You must learn to defer gratification," says the shrink his parents send him to.

"You must rise above frustration," says his tutor when math demons hoot in his ear.

"Why can spelling words break rules, but I can't?" he yells, banished to his room with *bite* and *knight, hose* and *clothes, phone* and *flown.*

When the pipe bomb Doc buys from one Marmaduke LaDough fails to explode at the museum, he's not surprised.

"Stuffed with sawdust. What'd I expect?" he tells his 300-pound cell-mate, who welcomes him with silk panties, and something else that he can't stand.

CRIMINAL MIND

This time it's a car the Reverend stole, a fishing trip he promised not to take, unsanctioned areolae he fervently kissed. If he can only stash the car in his garage, lock his out of-season brook trout in the trunk, spray enough Glade on his shirt to swamp gouts of Tabu. If he can only make it home in time for dinner, then whoever's waiting . . . Mom, wife, paramour . . . can't prove a thing.

Trouble is, a diapered toddler grabs his car keys and goes scooting through the motel parking lot.

The Reverend walks up cooing as if the brat is his beloved son, out for a post-Similac crawl.

The brat tries to run, but falls down and swallows the keys.

The Reverend grabs his neck and pretends to burp him, hissing, "Cough 'em up, milk-breath."

The Reverend knows that every character he dreams is part of him. Still, he squeezes until the brat spits up brown grasshopper tobacco, and finally those sinful, slimed-on keys.

AT THE STADIUM

Mobs break down the padlocked doors, though nothing's scheduled. The players are on strike. The owners have dissolved the teams.

Some fans clutch flags or Bibles. Others strain to read, through dusk and blowing leaves, their leather-bound Great Books.

Some play CDs of their parents' wisest words. Others spider-stomp parental CDs, and blare new ones by psychotherapists.

Many scrutinize road maps, but can't locate where they are or hoped to be. Most have forgotten when and how they came. They're hungry, but the hot dog stands are closed. Their bowels and bladders ache, but the toilets have been ripped out; the restrooms, boarded tight. No usher has been seen for years.

I hope a game occurs before the whole thing blows.

DEADBEATS' DAY

My mail-order Weather Wizard measures ninety-eight degrees, ninety-nine percent humidity as the red-white-and-blue Post Office truck grinds up.

In hopes I've won a prize, I slit the red envelope the mailman hands me, and read "YOUR FILE HAS BEEN ASSIGNED TO A COLLECTION AGENCY. HOWEVER, IN HONOR OF DEADBEAT'S DAY, WE WILL TELL THEM TO TAKE NO ACTION AGAINST YOU IF WE RECEIVE PAYMENT WITHIN ONE (1) WEEK."

The letter—signed "VINCENT GAMBINO," from the Icy Rash Cosmetics Company in Icy Rash, New York—goes on to say that I owe $57.03 for an 8-ounce "vile" of Icy Rash Cologne.

"So what I never ordered it?" I tell myself. "I'd better pay."

But I don't pay. I preserve each scarlet letter in a crystalline sheathe:

"Ten cents a week would spare us bankruptcy. We know you'll do what's right."

"We have the faith in you your mother never had, the harlot—or your dad, the disempowering douchebag."

"Pay us, or sunlight will crack and peel like paint. The wind will fall down writhing in the street. Never again will night smooth its jasmined washcloth down your thighs."

"Cough up, cheap bastard, or we'll crush your casaba and suck the seeds!"

"Oh God, we're sorry we were cross. Love made us lose control. We want so much to work this out. Bear with us, pretty please . . . "

I keep the letters in a hand-tooled Cordovan leather album that I bought by mail. It came, as promised, in two weeks, with an invoice I paid on Conscientious Debtor's Day.

ANHEDONIA IS NO LAUGHING MATTER

This Baltic principality was famed for its dour citizens long before the Russian blimp-of-gloom thumped down. While neighboring states excelled at yodeling-with-mouths-full and sex-on-skis, Anhedonians burned their strudel purposely, and perfected cross-country groaning. Kids filled their own stockings with coal on Christmas Eve, and plugged their chimneys to keep Santa outside. Sex was scorned, except to instigate childbirth, when women could bar husbands from the birth-room, and hog all the pain.

Winter never ends in Anhedonia. Kids can't heap up leaf-mountains to jump on—not that they'd want to—or chase stray leaves that crab-walk by. No one drops an armful down a winding slide, then skids after them shrieking. No one watches wood chips in a fountain circle like dreadnoughts, or plays pirate with stick-swords, attacking picnic-table galleons.

No one draws a wattled turkey in pink chalk on the sidewalk, then jumps up and down at all ecstatically.

ORGAN RECITAL

Well, of course, we had it tough.
— Monty Python

"My plantar fasciitis is so bad I can barely walk to my car."

"Your *car*? With my club feet, I have to crawl to the bathroom."

"At least you have feet. Diabetes chewed off mine."

"Easy Street! I have Lou Gehrig's disease."

"You'll live for years. My doctor gives me six months. In agony."

"Emphysema will kill me in three. Slow suffocation."

"Oh to have three months! I have three weeks."

"Fortunate Son! My heart won't last three days."

"I call that heaven. Cancer's drilled into my bones."

"I wish I had bones. Doctors extracted mine."

"*I* was born a lump of flesh and cartilage. Never had the pleasure of bones. I need a ventilator just to wheeze."

"You're lucky you can wheeze. I'm dead."

"I died three times, horribly. Last time, no one knew I'd revived, so they embalmed me. I felt every needle, every burning drop of formaldehyde. Then, when I was entirely dead, devils stuck me upside-down in a pot of boiling sewage full of alligators and piranha that will feast on me forever while worms burrow through my eyes, which still see everything."

"Luxury . . ."

III

TRUTH IN ADVERTISING

Any reasonable man would have assumed THREE BEDROOM APARTMENT, 600 PER MONTH. WON'T LAST! meant, "Grab it fast, before someone else does."

Nothing lasts, everyone knows. The potted roses he gave his wife for Valentine's, "guaranteed to brighten your home for years," turned brown and brittle before Mother's Day. Even the pencil stub that scratches his demand for a refund once stood eight inches tall, topped with an orange eraser-crown.

Who, though, would have expected a void in the exact spot his apartment used to be?

"Jen!" he calls his wife.

"Jason! Bree!" he calls his kids.

"Hermione!" he calls their new Chi-weenie pup.

No answer.

He's free.

I LOSE A NEW COLD WAR

Oleg from American Appliance Repair backs me up to where my washer squats, sour and clogged. He rumbles like a movie-monster, "What wrong with machine?"

He's twisting knobs as I explain. He hits his calculator. Hard. "One thirty forty-five to fix right now," he booms. "Make like brand new."

I should negotiate, I know. But Oleg looms. Behind him, Khrushchev pounds a table with his shoe. Men in fur hats squat on *The Bomb* as if it were a giant egg.

I barely dare to ask, "Is there a guarantee?"

"One year parts, tirty day labor."

"Is labor less reliable than parts?"

"One year parts, tirty day labor!" Oleg roars.

"Okay," I say to calm him. "Go ahead."

No thanks leave Oleg's lips. No, "Good. You won't be sorry." Only—all reverb and accusation—"How you pay?"

"Will a check do?"

Oleg frowns like a commissar considering gulag or firing squad, then growls, "Okay," and attacks the machine.

Five minutes later, he stabs a bill at me.

Lifting my check to the light, he squints to see if it is counterfeit, poisoned, or bugged, then crushes it into his pocket and, in wintery silence, stows his tools.

I squash an urge to praise Chekhov and Tchaikovsky, venturing instead, "How did you know what was wrong?"

Oleg scowls. Am I questioning his competence? Prying for trade secrets?

"Do you know your job?" he rumbles. "I know mine."

His steel-gray eyes shove me back to third grade, crouched under my desk. "Put your head between your legs," kids said, "and kiss your butt goodbye."

"You're like a doctor," I suggest. "You hear symptoms, and diagnose the disease." (Of course I'm fawning. International relations are at stake.)

Oleg snaps his tool box shut. "Somesing like dat," he growls, and rolls out of my house like the tanks I saw on black-and-white TV, then looked for *Hungry* in my stamp album, wondering how food ever squeezed through an Iron Curtain.

DWINDLEBAUM'S LAST STAND

He jams his foot into Time's elevator-door. Damned if he'll let the past slam shut behind him!

"Betrayers, begone!" he tells wrinkles that try to sneak onto his face. "Don't move," he tells each hair that starts to fall. "Stay where you are," he commands as seconds fail to slither by.

Brigitte Bardot in her prime appears. "I'm yours," she purrs. "Just step out of the door."

Dwindlebaum's heart strains toward her. The rest of him stays put.

His mother sets his favorite foods just out of reach on the floor: roast lamb with mint jelly, fresh green beans, a chocolate shake.

"I made this just for you," she says. "Please eat, honey. You're getting thin."

Tears scorch his cheeks. His stomach growls like a starved wolverine. But he won't budge.

Days and nights strobe-flash around him. Infants swell into adults, collapse into nursing homes, then melt to dust while, in the patch of sky above his head, the sun, like a golden bee stuck to blue flypaper, hoards its shrivel-juice and bides its time.

VENOMOUS MOUSE DISCOVERED
IN FARMER'S BARN

"You're a snake. Or a gila monster," other mice must have said.

"I'm not," the mouse (I'm guessing) said. "Really."

No one believed him, any more than people believe whacking a clogged salt-shaker merely clogs it more.

"The shock compacts the grains, immobilizing them," I told my Diner's Club, and proved it mathematically.

"So why does salt come out?" the diners yelled, and hurled baked potatoes at me.

I'd taken shelter in a nearby barn when I saw the mouse drop the farmer's pit bull with one bite.

For the next year, I met the mouse in secret, wearing leather gloves to feed him cheese.

"Danger makes life's fuse burn bright," I told my diary.

Chickadees seem to agree. The more danger, the more they *dee*. A pygmy owl evokes abundant *dee*s, while great horned owls—too big to mess with chickadees—call forth only one desultory *di*.

Macho Pig's chili cheese nacho that, by itself, can plug a human heart, gets not a peep. The venomous mouse, though, provokes so many *dee*s, it's a miracle he wasn't found before.

"What's the commotion, Mabel," Farmer Brown asks his wife one especially *dee*ful day.

"Darn chickadee's stuck again," she says.

"Give it a whack," Farmer Brown says, ceding the glory of discovery to me.

THE CARROT PUTSCH

Insurance salesman Louis Thrip becomes convinced that his fate is linked to carrots, which will help him in his trials.

He forces the word into sentences. "Pardon me, do you have the carrot—I mean *correct* time." "Sorry officer, I didn't see that red carrot."

He claims to feel "incomplete" away from carrots. He later adds "naked," "helpless," "at pain's mercy, of which it has none."

"Only carrots understand me," he declares.

He stuffs his pockets with them, hauls them in his briefcase, pulls them behind him in a wagon which he paints carrot-orange. He has one extra-fine specimen made into a pendant that never leaves his neck.

"You have coverage for your home and car," he tells clients. "Why not your carrots?"

He attacks grocery stores, and frees the carrots. He buys a bobsled, hitches carrots to it, and stands in his front yard shouting, "Mush!" He sleeps in pajamas of woven carrot fiber, and keeps a carrot under his pillow for protection.

Two wives and six girlfriends leave him because of "certain practices."

He's sure that life is grooming him for something big.

Currently, he's hiding in the Yucatán, trying to invent a better name than *Carrot Putsch* for what's now hiding up his sleeves.

FRENCH TOAST

Anthony Ambergris, CPA, returns to breakfast after a brief dyspeptic spell to find his French toast gone, his wife Annabel smirking adipose defiance from her blue flannel nightgown.

What can he do but pour syrup on the tablecloth, and eat?

"Spiteful turd," Annabel yells. "That's Belgian lace. It was a gift from my mother, whom you devour symbolically to injure me."

"I'm finishing my French toast," Anthony explains. "I was promised French toast, and the world must not be let to break its promises, or it will grow into a pimple-faced delinquent without morals or respect."

"Which it's already done, doddering asshole," Annabel rails.

"Which, if you use language like that in front of it, how can it help but be?" Anthony cries.

AN END TO ORATORY

Senator Wafflehouse jets home from Cannes to find that his TV won't work without his wife's okay. His best pants will not unzip. His coffee pot spits in his eye. His Ford Mustang rears like a bronco, then stalls, nickering.

"My life-coach said, *Take back your power*," Mrs. W states.

"Fine. Laudable. But not by treachery," Wafflehouse cries. "Treachery will spring back and eat the hand that bites it . . . feed the hand that eats it . . . no, wait . . ."

He dials for help. The phone sprays sewage in his ear.

He tries to run. The rug rolls under him like a treadmill.

A speech springs to his lips. He clamps it between his teeth, and leaps onto a stump-sized table to deliver it.

The table tilts and dumps him on the floor.

"Teach him about *just desserts*," Mrs. W commands the carpet: rough with taste buds, slick with drool.

HUNGRY

When, after hard and bloody labor, a baby shoves its way into the world, the ob-gyn is stunned to find no afterbirth.

"Did he eat it?" a nurse asks. "Look at those teeth."

The baby leaps for Momma's breast. She needs stitches when the lactation coach pries him away. "Some babies do best on formula," the coach admits.

This baby thrives on formula—gallons of it. When it's all gone, he eats the rubber nipple, then the glass bottle.

"A real go-getter!" gloats Dad.

Baby eats the b'anky Aunt Gayle knitted, with his birth-date and eight embroidered sheep. He eats his mattress, guaranteed for fifteen years. He eats the crib his grandma air-freighted from France.

"He isn't fat. He's husky," Mom insists.

"A take-no-prisoners guy," Dad proclaims. "He'll be a CEO before he's 35."

The next day, Baby eats them both. He eats his room, and then the house. He's starting on the yard when Social Services arrive.

He eats the social worker's forms, then her car, with her caterwauling inside.

He eats the house next door—ornamental brick sidewalk and all. He eats the whole block, including the street. He eats the city, then the state, the country, the continent.

He drinks the oceans, and chomps the earth like a cheese-ball.

He eats the stars, the galaxies, the space between. He eats until there's nothing left.

"Waaa!" he cries, "Waaa!"—and eats the tangy nothingness. He eats until only one speck remains, smaller than the tip of a quark-sized pin.

He gapes his mouth for that.

A Big Bang begins.

TROUBLING SOUNDS

I wake to a loud *Uhhn!*, then a dull *Whump!*

The pre-dawn light is just enough to see, on the lawn outside my new apartment, a woman shot-putting in a bikini that could make a dozen of the ones Misty and Kerri rocked when they won beach volleyball gold. This woman spins, the silver shot tucked under her neck as if, add water, it becomes a violin.

I want to charge outside and tell her, "Keep it down." But she's gone before I can get dressed.

Outside my classroom at the U, she's there again. Students laugh. (At her or me?) I end class early, driven out by *Uhhn!*s and *Whump!*s.

I take my daughter, Chloe, to the beach. Someone was killed by a great white, so we have to stay on shore.

"Are you a manatee or a mouse?" a boy asks me when Chloe, having buried me in sand, starts to build a sand hospital for "the poor eaten man." The boy and Chloe ignore the shot-putter when she lumbers up, lugging her shot in a mesh sling.

Soon it's *Uhhn! Whump!* very near my head.

Am I the only one who hears? Who sees?

I take my E-harmony date to India's Flavors: chicken tika for her, lamb vindaloo for me, garlic naan and a mango lassi to share. Before we've scarfed two bites, the shot-putter thumps into the parking lot.

Unnh! Whump!

Did my ex-wife send her to spy? Could she *be* my ex-wife? We only talk, these days, by phone. She says she's "gained a little weight," and is "pursuing new interests."

"That woman keeps looking at you," Ms Harmony says. "Are you her coach?"

"No! I hardly know her."

"Hardly as in erection?"

"As in *barely."*

"Barely as in naked?"

Where but downhill could the night roll from there?

SECOND SON

Can my son ride with yours? I'm scared of trains.
— Blonde woman in a blue dress

His name is Nathan, but we call him Nate as the Enchanted Railroad's miniature train puffs away from Descanso Gardens station.

Our first-born, Evan, bonks Nate with a Ninja Turtle, and brains him with a plastic baseball bat. Yet by the time we pass the first crossing—soprano bell pinging, quarter-sized red light flashing as park-goers wave—the boys, in fourth and third grade, stand as one against the world.

Before we reach the rhododendrons, where a fountain blasts like a sprung water-main, Evan has made the National Honor Society. Nate has taken up shoplifting and general thuggery.

As our train chuffs through the woods beside an artificial creek where koi hang, gold fins fluttering, Evan enters UCLA (English major). When Nate chooses the army over jail, the Descanso Engineer—80 if he's a millisecond—toots three times on his Enchanted Railroad horn.

We pass the Wishing Well where kids drop pennies on a sunken garden gnome as Evan graduates *summa cum,* and starts teaching Composition part-time at four colleges.

Cited for bravery in the Middle East, Nate is honorably discharged as orange daisies smile and sway.

Inside the Tunnel of Trees—still hung, in June, with Christmas lights—Evan marries a heart surgeon, and lands a tenure-track at Glendale Community College on the same day Nate's one-man show of watercolors opens at Kreisler Gallery.

As the second crossing-bell frantically pings, its light flashing ambulance-red, Evan's wife runs off with her (female) anesthesiologist, leaving Evan to raise their son, Ezra, alone.

Two oak trees later, Nate meets a Hungarian juggler. At the koi pond, they have a baby girl, then give her up for adoption.

The boys have grown apart. Nate feels we favor Evan, so we downplay our pride when, as the train slows entering the Walk of Roses, Evan publishes a novel about a dad whose doctor-wife leaves him for a lesbian from outer space.

Refusing our help, Nate puts himself through night school and, in front of the Frog Fountain, renounces Art to become a CPA. When we reach the station three days from his 29th birthday, he jumps off before the train completely stops and, with a gray-haired woman in a dress of lupine-blue, walks away without so much as a goodbye.

THE BURN

My son said his first word, *proboscismonkey,* at the zoo when a big-nosed granny leaned over his pram.

Twenty-three years later, he said it instead of "Sure," when asked to join the Pittsburgh Post-Mod Orchestra as First Anti-violin.

Resignation asked Sorrow to the prom. "Sorry," she said, "Petulance has a nicer car."

Forced to work Thanksgiving, the nurse injected the Turkish patient with gravy.

Just when warmth seemed unattainable as Yap Island on a mechanic's creeper, the sun set down its picnic basket, and spread its gold shawl over the field's shivering knees.

If a lungfish can trek from Queensland to Lenice Lake, maybe our marriage-pigeon can fly home. Maybe the dead dog of our love will sit and beg.

One day it's winter; six months later, miraculously, not.
"Ba-DA," I cry, shaking my knuckles in Death's face. "Ba-DA! Ba-DA!" I scream, flexing and unflexing. Going for the burn.

PORTUGUESE MAN-OF-WAR

1.

The Portuguese Man-of-War is a large, warm-water jellyfish that floats on the ocean by means of a translucent gas-filled balloon, streaked iridescent like oily water in the sun. Below this float-balloon hangs a mass of multi-colored guts, and many blue, red, and purple tentacles for stinging prey.

Seen at a distance, the float brings to mind a sailing ship, hence its name, though its shape is more nearly like the top half of a Roman helmet, or the head of a nearly submerged, crested dinosaur.

2.

Around March 1, before the spring crowd, Teddy Liedeker and I loved to go to Galveston. While our families grilled sand-burgers, we'd comb miles of beach to see what winter had tossed up. There'd be old bottles, light bulbs, net-floats, shells, crates with foreign writing, driftwood—sometimes whole trees—plus an occasional dead shark, grouper, sea turtle, or nameless rotting monster inches deep in flies. Not to mention Man-of-Wars. March was their month.

We'd grab long sticks and gallop up and down the shore like knights, lancing balloons to hear them pop. They were made of a thin jello that dried brittle in the sun. When one washed in, we'd wade out, poke our sticks behind it, and lift ten feet of tentacle. Being heavier, tentacles trailed the balloons, so we were safe. We hoped. On shore or off, we never walked behind a Man-of-War. Even the popped balloons spit out a mist that reddened our legs, and itched to beat all hell.

3.

Looking up *plesiosaur* in the *Brittanica*, I came across Portuguese Man-of-War. Some facts:

The Man-of-War is not a true jellyfish, but a complex colony of polyps, each adapted to one function: protection/food capture, digestion, flotation, reproduction.

The Man-of-War was named by English sailors who encountered flotillas of them in the seas off Portugal.

Man-of-War tenacles may exceed fifteen feet long. Their sting can kill a man. The best antidote is vinegar.

The Man-of-War's balloon may be a foot long. The animal secretes the gas inside: 90 percent nitrogen, a trace of argon, the rest oxygen. A valve allows gas to escape, and the balloon to sink as much as necessary, when necessary.

The Man-of-War moves solely by current or wind, its balloon doubling as a sail. It slows its speed by releasing gas and sinking. The Man-of-War's shape causes it to tack 45 degrees into the wind. In the northern hemisphere, it tacks to the left; in the southern, to the right.

Sea turtles are one of the few animals that eat Man-of-Wars. Their shells and scales protect them, but they have to feed with their eyes closed.

The Man-of-War Fish lives among the tentacles, safe from enemies, sharing food killed by the Man-of-War, and browsing on its tentacles. Healthy, the fish is immune to Man-of-War venom. Becoming sick or injured, it falls prey at once.

4.

There are always Man-of-Wars around Galveston. They're rare except in March, though, and you usually see them coming. Even so, half-blind as I am without glasses, I never swim or surf without a friend to scan the waves. I remember too well my father's tan face, stark white against the sand, my mother frantic, me shrieking, thinking he was dead.'

The rows of fiery welts on his back and legs lasted into the next spring.

5.

I just heard a lecture called "Confusion in Sexual Identity: the Search for a Model." If I was ever confused that way, it stopped on my fifth birthday.

I was sitting on Dad's shoulders, surf-fishing and jumping waves, both of us in swim trunks. I saw a rainbow-balloon float by and started to tell Dad, just as he flinched once and, without even scaring me, waded fifty yards to shore and gently set me down.

EAR-BETTER EMPORIUM

The waiting room looks larger than the baseball field where, in 1888, "Dummy" Hoy introduced hand-signals to the major leagues.

Some patients speak in sign language. Some scream in one another's ears.

I've come because rock music smashed line drives into my eardrums six nights a week for twenty years. Now a wall of whine has trapped me: tinny tinnitus, relentless as death. Unlikely to end in even one great symphony.

Patients could hold their own World Series in this room. The blinking sign—LISTEN HARD. YOU CAN'T SEE THE DOCTOR IF YOU DON'T HEAR YOUR NAME—could call us to our appointments when it's not full of cartoon ear-trumpets hurled skyward to celebrate home runs.

Who, if the umpire speaks softly, will argue his "Strike three"?

MAGIC MOUNTAIN

"Magic Mountain Pkwy—2 miles," the green sign jeers. There's barely time to veer far right, and claim last place in a line of cars that seems stopped dead. Still, slow as a fault, we grind ahead.

"It's taking years," our son Ben whines.

"Griping won't help," Trudi reminds.

"Do you have an appointment?" I demand.

Trudi's driving, so I pry off my shoes and study *How To Pick Up Hotties*. I've changed its cover for one lettered, in real gold, *Holy Bible*. Too late I see that *Bible* is spelled *Bubble*. Good thing Trudi's occupied by Hayseed Doughie crooning "China Squirrel."

"To pick up a hottie," I read, "attach handles when she's lying down. If she's not lying, ask her to."

All nearby cars house dioramas—*Washington Crosses the Tupperware. Lou Gehrig's Farewell Screech*—or is daylight playing tricks as, sun plunging, we reach PARK HERE?

My wallet leaves my pocket with a sweaty *schwuck*.

"Twenty clams to stow our Dodge Ram while they fleece us," Trudi groans.

Ben—hearing roller-coasters roar, riders shrieking too far off to see—cries, "That's recorded. I'll bet there *are* no rides."

"How does that speculation help us?" Trudi sighs.

Ben totters, glassy-eyed, out of our car, then plops sunny-side-up on the pavement. I luggage-nudge him forward to a booth where I get dinged $119.85 (coupon-reduced from $119.97), then have to *taekwando* our way into the park.

It's almost dark as we stagger toward a line marked *Breath of Death*. We've seen it on TV: riders in coffins keening as they rim the eye-holes of a skull.

Beanied with snow, a mountain magically appears. Pteranodons circle its summit, lit up by a neon sign: MAGIC MOUNTAIN IS NOW CLOSED. HAVE A NICE DAY.

"Don't tease the birdy," Trudi shrills as a pteranodon grabs Ben by his suspenders, and lifts.

A MAN WALKS INTO A POLLUTED POND

and trots out with a horse-penis in place of his own.

His wife is pleased, and tells a friend, who tells her husband, who dives into the pond and scampers out with the penis of a tree-shrew.

A bitter bachelor tries to drown himself, and hops out with a huge dong and soft gray pubic fur. "Rabbit, I think," he tells the gathering mob. "A BIG rabbit."

Tree-shrew-penis—fearing to go home—screams, "Better pecker," leaps back into the pond, and capers out wagging the schlong of a giraffe.

The mob of men crowding around the pond charge in, laughing and splashing. Seconds later, they've become whole animals: goats, horses, pigs, gerbils, tortoises, iguanas . . .

"Turn back!" a mouse-man squeaks.

The crush is too strong. Even wild squealing from pig-man can't prevent the lemming-plunge, which doesn't cease until the pond is dry as Atacama sand.

The town's remaining grown-ups—all women—fence off the pond-bed and cart in animal feed.

"Thank the Lord," the ladies say. "We prefer a petting zoo."

A CERTAIN PEAR

is juicy, sweet, and confident the day she drops into the grocer's bin. One by one, though—by chance, really—others are bought, while she is left behind.

Brown spots fester in her crisp white flesh. Her golden skin wrinkles and cracks.

She harangues shoppers, "Beauty is skin-deep. My bruises have more vitamins than all these hussies with their perfect curves combined."

But since pears speak in clusters of silence, no one is convinced. And finally a pimpled stock-boy grabs her by the stem and tosses her, silently shrieking, into the trash.

It's just a short ride to the dump.

Three days and nights she lies there, wedged between a crusty hambone and an old brassiere. Then, just at sunset, a winged cabbage appears. There's not a dry eye in the dump as the pear is entered into the Glorious Order of Decaying Things. All she has to do is lie back and enjoy as, one by one, her atoms squiggle off to re-construct the world.

SACRED GRAPES

There is the usual luggage-banging, the standard fidgeting and babble, then the hiss of the Greyhound's door, a hush, and a tortoise wearing a visored driver's cap clumps aboard.

"What's that?" a fat lady in Aisle 3, Seat 1 demands as the passengers all stare.

"A giant turtle, stupid," her 10-year-old son declares.

The tortoise heaves itself into the driver's seat. Its elephant-legs don't reach the clutch-pedal or brake. Its shell keeps vibrating off the seat when it finally, with its thick, clawed paws, manages to turn the engine on.

"I took this bus to escape animal husbandry," a pretty farm-girl wails. "It isn't fair!"

"Oh life is vicious, life is tough," an old man keens from the rear.

The farm-girl first, then all the passengers pick up the chant, rolling the words over and over on their tongues like sacred grapes they've spent their whole lives looking for.

THE IMPEDERS

Too fat to climb, they must be dragged in cushioned litters to the pyramid's peak, where they rest, guzzling our hard-earned beer. Our daughters, bare breasts swaying, smooth cool water on their shaved pates as we slave beneath Ra's fiery eye.

Sometimes, for fun and to justify their princely salaries, they make us hoist huge granite blocks with our pinkies. Then we must prove the rocks are granite—not sandstone, say, or feldspar—by sacrificing a bullock (sometimes a buttock) to the gods. Whatever the gods say, Impeders get the meat.

To keep us on our toes, they debate, not Pharaoh's right to three-fourths of our GNP, but the ethnic balance of our slave corps, if our work songs give offense, if the ankh and flail are properly inscribed on the invoices that certify each block was hewn from the right spot, dragged in the right style by the right men with the right rites performed by the proper priests, overseen themselves by bejeweled Impeders, each of whom has his own scribe to write, with a diamond stylus, Yea or Nay.

At the least transgression of the Law Eternal, which Impeders re-write every day, they all place silver whistles to their lips, and squeal, whereon work stops (but not the squealing) while the High Council decides what must be razed and built anew.

Thus we lift ourselves above the bawling tribes who, in their ignorance, attack our borders, steal our grain and gold, slaughter our soldiers, and enslave and breed our women with no consideration beyond if, and at what price, they will succeed.

DR. BIRD

Gaspar identifies, even with her head bitten off, the towhee that flapped into his house on Easter, slamming into walls until he trapped her in a blanket, ran her outside—warm, quivering, resigned as Jesus—then watched her climb toward heaven on stubby brown wings.

"Alas, poor Towhee," he says to mock what the world calls his "over-sensitivity." He'd heave the dead body onto the hill behind his house, but a doe is nibbling poison ivy there, skittish, afraid of predators. So the bird stays in the flowerbed where she lies.

Ants and beetles hollow her. Sunshine dries her into a brown shuttlecock.

"Is that dead bird still out there?" Gaspar's wife demands.

"*I* don't know," Gaspar says, though he checks every morning, first thing. "Hello," he says, and thinks, despite her lack of head, he hears "Hi" back.

As a joke, he asks, "Dr. Bird—should I divorce my wife for preferring wiener-dogs to kids?"

No response.

A week later, he asks, "Dr. Bird—should I wear my white dress shirt, or risk the lavender?"

Not a word from Dr. Bird.

Then one day, as spring flutters toward summer, and orioles nest in the guava tree, Dr. Bird snits, "You think they're prettier than me."

Each time Gaspar fills the hummingbirds' feeder, Dr. Bird snorts, "Hmmph!"

In June, as mockingbirds fill the air with mimicked tunes, Dr. Bird whines, "I know you wish that *I* could sing."

When a freak cloudburst hits in July, Gaspar doesn't dare bring Dr. Bird inside. Even so, his wife declares, "Philanderer, I'm leaving you."

Once she's gone, Gaspar pulls Dr. Bird out of a mound of soggy leaves.

"Forgive me," he says. But she's not listening any more.

A NOTE ON THE TYPE

L-Hepatic type was born in Antwerp, Belgium, 1938, and moved to Houston, Texas at the start of World War II. First featured in the G.I. favorite *Mary Jo Forsure,* it took the post-war USA by storm, appearing in such books as *Seismography for Singles, The Big Little Book of Skin-Lightening,* and *Disemboweling Dan.*

Its dream to be the type of choice for baseball columnists was never realized, though it appeared in a truss ad opposite a picture of Willy Mays.

A long affair with a type known only as "RD" ended badly when RD merged with Helvetica. L-Hepatic's mood darkened after that. It aspired to *Oedipus* and *Lear,* but typesetters thought it "best-suited for an absurdist touch."

Among its memorable lines:

Let a dog's barking light your way.

My voice fails me; I can't say why.

Smoking causes colon cancer? Hell, some people don't know how to smoke.

Honors include the Wallace Beaverburn Award, and the prestigious Ralph and Mary Dollop Prize.

Used rarely in the twenty-first century, L-Hepatic nearly perished in a linotype fire in Alvin, Texas, August 2010, but was rescued by poet Randolph Sunscreen Pricklypear who, before his untimely smothering, used the type in each of his self-published books, and swore never to marry until "universal acclaim frees up my energy for love."

ENCORE

Hunched at his desk, an author struggles to describe how, when applause has lasted long enough, a guitarist curvy as her instrument glides from behind red velvet curtains and re-seats herself on a black stool. Crossing her left leg carefully over her right, she unscrews the former at the knee, heaves it into the crowd, and starts to play.

At this point, the phone rings with such conviction that the author jerks it up.

"Squirrel Hit-Men are the new Vampire Teens," his agent shouts.

"You mean *girl* hit-men?"

"Oscar time!" the agent roars.

Back at his desk, the author tries to describe how the guitarist hops offstage, then, when applause draws her back, unscrews her right leg at the knee, and tosses it to the crowd. Finished playing, she stumps offstage with dignity despite her black gown's puddling, then is called back and, like a gymnast mounting the pommel horse, re-takes her seat.

The author explains the artful way, on subsequent encores, she tosses to the crowd her thighs, head, neck, torso, and pelvis (discreetly sheathed), then her left hand, forearm, and upper arm, each time playing better than before.

The phone clamors again. The author yanks it up.

"Don't forget the Fry Concept," his agent screams. "The Hero's Gurney."

"*High concept*? Hero's *journey*?"

"Walk of Fame, baby!" the agent roars.

Re-settling into his chair, the author describes how the guitarist's right arm floats offstage, then, as applause shakes the stadium, floats back, the guitar floating up to meet it and create, as the arm blips away, *sounds too ravishing for words.*

The author hates the way that phrase admits defeat. He tries, "beautiful as a New Guinea sunset on bird of paradise wings," "delectable as honey-bell tangerines floating in ambrosial seas," "mellifluous as *Sir Percy Persiflage of the Antipodes*," then scratches out all three.

Squid-like describes the guitarist's hand as it swims into the spotlight before the index finger curls to touch the thumb, and the whole hand blips away.

Next, the audience blips away; then, the author; then, the guitar. Sounds Pythagoras might have called *music of the spheres* fill the concert hall, empty now as the darkness between stars.

REPORT

Now that Boredom and Depression are punishable by stiff fines, half paid to the accuser, there has been a marked increase in applications for treatment. Even those die-hards who cling to their affliction like a winning Lotto ticket have been forced to, as the song says, "Put on a Happy Face." Society is thus spared visual contamination, though undetected carriers still spread ennui.

The enemy is, as always, Ignorance. Many of the afflicted, especially those in rural areas, have no idea that "B & D" are caused by microviruses with, respectively, sighing and grimacing faces. Imagine the sufferers' delight to learn that their disease can be prevented by wearing toy space helmets, and cured by medication made from molecules shaped like grinning game-show hosts.

Each week sees new strides in detection. The conviction/arrest ratio steadily climbs. Fumigation is required in known trouble spots; and the number of such spots increases daily.

Soon everyone will be interested and happy.

DUMMY LOVE

Is it her bosomy construction, or the sorrow in her blue disk-eyes that draws Sam's gaze to where she lies, limp as a paralytic, among chattering teeth, flies-in-ice-cubes, and fake vomit in the window of Snickering Hedgehog Novelties?

"Ventriloquism's a big, honking waste of time," Sam's wife Janni opines. But when the dummy squeaks, "Golly-wolly, hot tamale!" as she bounces by in her booster bra, she has to grin.

"We should laugh more," she says. So Sam makes the dummy tell jokes: "Three executioners take flying lessons . . ." "A man walks into a wood-chipper . . ."

When, by mistake, Sam slams a door on the dummy's plastic thumb, Janni laughs so hard she chokes.

"Once you and I were lace jellies caressing in tropical seas," she tells Sam.

"Once we were ospreys trading kelp bass in mid-air," Sam replies.

Thrusting their hands under the dummy's gingham dress, they use her hands to caress each other.

"Homewrecker!" Janni shrills, and slaps the dummy's wistful smile.

"She's nothing to me!" Sam insists, and kicks the dummy's squishy chest.

"I love you," the dummy sighs, shapely and wistful as before.

"Did you make her say that?" Janni asks.

"No," Sam says. "Did you?"

ABOUT THE AUTHOR

Recipient of grants from the Whiting and Guggenheim foundations, Charles Harper Webb's latest collection of poems, *Sidebend World,* was published by the University of Pittsburgh Press. Webb recently won the Longleaf Press Editor's Choice Award for his collection, *Old Gnu,* forthcoming in 2026. He has worked as a professional rock singer/guitarist, a psychotherapist, and is Professor emeritus of English at California State University, Long Beach.

ACKNOWLEDGMENTS

The author would like to thank the editors of the following publications for first publishing these poems, sometimes with other titles and in other versions:

Chiron Review: "Deadbeat's Day," Dinner with the Blithervilles," "Dwindlebaum's Last Stand, "Dummy Love," "Fyodor," "Ivy-Covered Monkey," "The Impeders"
Conté: "Secrets of the Body Revealed"
DMQ Review: "Esquire," "The Elephant of Surprise"
Fiction International: "A Man Walks Into a Polluted Pond," "Criminal Mind," "Familiarity," "Man Tries to Blow Up Museum of Tolerance" "Pharaoh Thanks God for the Exodus"
Harpur Palate: "Warthog Podiatry"
Heavy Feather Review: "An End to Oratory," "At the Stadium"
I-70 Review: "Halloween"
In Posse Review: "The Sky Rains Blood"
Indiana Review: "Mr. Twig"
Jung Journal: "The New Machines," "The Secret of My Success"
Moon City Review: "Half in Love with Easeful Death," "Hungry"
Nerve Cowboy: "In the Hall of Wasted Quesadillas:
Plume Anthology: "A Working Class Gyro" "College of Babies," "Kindness Detector," "Truth in Advertising"
Prairie Schooner: "I Lose a New Cold War"
Quarterly West: "Replacement People," "Surprise"
Rhino: "A Jealous Dad," "Dr. Bird"
Sentence: "Instant Baby," "Organ Recital"
TriQuarterly: "Magic Mountain"
Verdad: "I Love Her So Madly"
Vox Populi: "Department of Discontent"
Wormwood Review: "A Situation of Extreme Hopelessness," "Portuguese Man of War," "Sacred Grapes"

"Second Son" was published in the anthology *Bear Flag Republic*, Editor Christopher Buckley, Greenhouse Review Press, Alcatraz Editions, 2008
"The Gold Standard" was published in the anthology *In the Black / In the Red*, Editors Vando & Miller, Helicon Nine Editions, 2012
"Handsome Can Sit Up By Himself" was published in the anthology *A Cast-Iron Aeroplane That Can Actually Fly*, Editor Peter Johnson, MadHat Press, 2019.

Special thanks to, alphabetically, Ron Koertge, Eric Morago, Karen Schneider, and William Trowbridge for invaluable editorial assistance, and to Edward Hirsch, who got the train on track.

The writing of this book was partially funded by California State University, Long Beach Scholarly and Creative Activities Awards.

Also Available from Moon Tide Press

Outliving Michael, Steven Reigns (2025)
Prayers with a Side of Cash, Kathleen Florence (2025)
Somewhere, a Playground, Rich Ferguson (2025)
The Tautology of Water, Giovanni Boskovich (2025)
Take Care, Mark Danowsky (2025)
Dilapitatia, Kelly Gray (2025)
Reluctant Prophets, J.D. Isip (2025)
Enormous Blue Umbrella, Donna Hilbert (2025)
Sky Leaning Toward Winter, Terri Niccum (2024)
Living the Sundown: A Caregiving Memoir, G. Murray Thomas (2024)
Figure Study, Kathryn de Lancellotti (2024)
Suffer for This: Love, Sex, Marriage, & Rock 'N' Roll,
       Victor D. Infante (2024)
What Blooms in the Dark, Emily J. Mundy (2024)
Fable, Bryn Wickerd (2024)
Diamond Bars 2, David A. Romero (2024)
Safe Handling, Rebecca Evans (2024)
More Jerkumstances: New & Selected Poems, Barbara Eknoian (2024)
Dissection Day, Ally McGregor (2023)
He's a Color Until He's Not, Christian Hanz Lozada (2023)
The Language of Fractions, Nicelle Davis (2023)
Paradise Anonymous, Oriana Ivy (2023)
Now You Are a Missing Person, Susan Hayden (2023)
Maze Mouth, Brian Sonia-Wallace (2023)
Tangled by Blood, Rebecca Evans (2023)
Another Way of Loving Death, Jeremy Ra (2023)
Kissing the Wound, J.D. Isip (2023)
Feed It to the River, Terhi K. Cherry (2022)
Beat Not Beat: An Anthology of California Poets Screwing
      on the Beat and Post-Beat Tradition (2022)
When There Are Nine: Poems Celebrating the Life and Achievements
      of Ruth Bader Ginsburg (2022)
The Knife Thrower's Daughter, Terri Niccum (2022)
2 Revere Place, Aruni Wijesinghe (2022)

Here Go the Knives, Kelsey Bryan-Zwick (2022)
Trumpets in the Sky, Jerry Garcia (2022)
Threnody, Donna Hilbert (2022)
A Burning Lake of Paper Suns, Ellen Webre (2021)
Instructions for an Animal Body, Kelly Gray (2021)
Head *V* Heart: New & Selected Poems, Rob Sturma (2021)
*Sh!t Men Say to Me: A Poetry Anthology in Response
        to Toxic Masculinity* (2021)
Flower Grand First, Gustavo Hernandez (2021)
Everything is Radiant Between the Hates, Rich Ferguson (2020)
When the Pain Starts: Poetry as Sequential Art, Alan Passman (2020)
This Place Could Be Haunted If I Didn't Believe in Love,
        Lincoln McElwee (2020)
Impossible Thirst, Kathryn de Lancellotti (2020)
Lullabies for End Times, Jennifer Bradpiece (2020)
Crabgrass World, Robin Axworthy (2020)
Contortionist Tongue, Dania Ayah Alkhouli (2020)
The only thing that makes sense is to grow, Scott Ferry (2020)
Dead Letter Box, Terri Niccum (2019)
Tea and Subtitles: Selected Poems 1999-2019, Michael Miller (2019)
At the Table of the Unknown, Alexandra Umlas (2019)
The Book of Rabbits, Vince Trimboli (2019)
Everything I Write Is a Love Song to the World, David McIntire (2019)
Letters to the Leader, HanaLena Fennel (2019)
Darwin's Garden, Lee Rossi (2019)
Dark Ink: A Poetry Anthology Inspired by Horror (2018)
Drop and Dazzle, Peggy Dobreer (2018)
Junkie Wife, Alexis Rhone Fancher (2018)
The Moon, My Lover, My Mother, & the Dog, Daniel McGinn (2018)
Lullaby of Teeth: An Anthology of Southern California Poetry (2017)
Angels in Seven, Michael Miller (2016)
A Likely Story, Robbi Nester (2014)
Embers on the Stairs, Ruth Bavetta (2014)
The Green of Sunset, John Brantingham (2013)
The Savagery of Bone, Timothy Matthew Perez (2013)
The Silence of Doorways, Sharon Venezio (2013)
Cosmos: An Anthology of Southern California Poetry (2012)

Straws and Shadows, Irena Praitis (2012)
In the Lake of Your Bones, Peggy Dobreer (2012)
I Was Building Up to Something, Susan Davis (2011)
Hopeless Cases, Michael Kramer (2011)
One World, Gail Newman (2011)
What We Ache For, Eric Morago (2010)
Now and Then, Lee Mallory (2009)
Pop Art: An Anthology of Southern California Poetry (2009)
In the Heaven of Never Before, Carine Topal (2008)
A Wild Region, Kate Buckley (2008)
Carving in Bone: An Anthology of Orange County Poetry (2007)
Kindness from a Dark God, Ben Trigg (2007)
A Thin Strand of Lights, Ricki Mandeville (2006)
Sleepyhead Assassins, Mindy Nettifee (2006)
Tide Pools: An Anthology of Orange County Poetry (2006)
Lost American Nights: Lyrics & Poems, Michael Ubaldini (2006)

Patrons

Moon Tide Press would like to thank the following people for their support in helping publish the finest poetry from the Southern California region. To sign up as a patron, visit www.moontidepress.com or send an email to publisher@moontidepress.com.

Anonymous
Robin Axworthy
Conner Brenner
Nicole Connolly
Bill Cushing
Susan Davis
Kristen Baum DeBeasi
Peggy Dobreer
Kate Gale
Dennis Gowans
Alexis Rhone Fancher
HanaLena Fennel
Half Off Books & Brad T. Cox
Donna Hilbert
Jim & Vicky Hoggatt
Michael Kramer
Ron Koertge & Bianca Richards
Gary Jacobelly
Ray & Christi Lacoste

Jeffery Lewis
Zachary & Tammy Locklin
Lincoln McElwee
David McIntire
José Enrique Medina
Michael Miller & Rachanee Srisavasdi
Michelle & Robert Miller
Ronny & Richard Morago
Terri Niccum
Andrew November
Jeremy Ra
Luke & Mia Salazar
Jennifer Smith
Roger Sponder
Andrew Turner
Rex Wilder
Mariano Zaro
Wes Bryan Zwick

www.ingramcontent.com/pod-product-compliance
Lightning Source LLC
Chambersburg PA
CBHW031142090426
42738CB00008B/1187